Yoga, Hatha-Yoga and Raja-Yoga

By
Annie Besant

Copyright © 2020 Lamp of Trismegistus. All rights reserved. No part of this publication may be reproduced or transmitted in any form or by any means, electronic or mechanical, including photocopying, recording, or by any information storage and retrieval system, without permission in writing from Lamp of Trismegistus. Reviewers may quote brief passages.

ISBN: 978-1-63118-476-5

Esoteric Classics

Other Books in this Series and Related Titles

The Hymns of Hermes by G. R. S. Mead (978-1-63118-405-5)

Buddhist Psalms by Shinran (978-1-63118-465-9)

Gnosis of the Mind by G. R. S. Mead (978-1-63118-408-6)

Clairvoyance and Psychic Abilities by A Besant &c (978-1-63118-403-1)

Atma Bodha & Tattva Bodha by Adi Shankara &c (978-1-63118-401-7)

A Collection of Early Writings on Astral Travel (978-1-63118-477-2)

The Path of Light: A Manual of Maha-Yana Buddhism (978-1-63118-471-0)

Catholicism, Yoga and Hinduism by Hartmann &c (978-1-63118-478-9)

The Golden Verses of Pythagoras: Five Translations (978-1-63118-479-6)

Tao Te Ching by Lao Tzu & Charles Johnston (978-1-63118-402-4)

The Book of the Watchers by Enoch (978-1-63118-416-1)

The Hymn of Jesus by G. R. S. Mead (978-1-63118-492-5)

Confessions of an English Opium-Eater by T De Quincey (978-1-63118-485-7)

Qabbalistic Teachings and the Tree of Life by M P Hall (978-1-63118-482-6)

Rosicrucian Rules, Secret Signs, Codes and Symbols by various (978-1-63118-488-8)

The Sepher Yetzirah and the Qabalah by M P Hall (978-1-63118-481-9)

History and Teachings of the Rosicrucians by W W Westcott &c (978-1-63118-487-1)

The Poem of Hashish by A Crowley & C Baudelaire (978-1-63118-484-0)

The Machinery of the Mind by Dion Fortune (978-1-63118-451-2)

The Star and the Garter by Aleister Crowley (978-1-63118-406-2)

The Leadbeater Reader: A Selection of Occult Essays (978-1-63118-483-3)

Audio versions are also available on Audible, Amazon and Apple

Table of Contents

Introduction...7

Yoga
By Annie Besant...9

The Hatha-Yoga and Raja-Yoga of India
By Annie Besant...41

INTRODUCTION

The word "esoteric" can be difficult to define. Esotericism in general can be seen less as a system of beliefs and more as a category, which encompasses numerous, different systems of beliefs. It's a bit of juxtaposition, since the word "esoteric" indicates something that few people know about, while the term itself broadly covers numerous philosophies, practices, areas of study and belief systems.

In a greater sense, Esotericism acts as a storehouse for secret knowledge, which is often considered ancient *(by tradition, if not by fact),* passed down from generation to generation, in private. At various times in history, simply possessing the knowledge of some of these subjects, was considered illegal and a jailable offence, if discovered. This usually included such general topics as Alchemy, Pharmacology, Qabalah, Hermeticism, Occultism, Ceremonial Magic, Astrology, Divination, Rosicrucianism and so on. Collectively, these areas of study were often referred to as the esoteric sciences.

Sometimes, the outer garment of a subject isn't esoteric, while what is hidden beneath it, is. As an example, Freemasonry isn't necessarily esoteric by nature (at *least not anymore),* but certain signs, passwords and handshakes given to the candidate during their initiation, are in fact, esoteric, in the sense that they are hidden from the general public.

Today, in the twenty-first century, such topics are readily available at bookstores across the country, and numerous mainsteam publishers offer beginners guides and coffee-table volumes on many of these subjects, intended for mass appeal. Books like *"The Secret"* have turned previously arcane topics into household knowledge. All that being the case, however, it isn't to say that there still aren't buried secrets to uncover, ancient wisdom being ignored and forgotten mysteries to be explored. In fact, it is often that we are only able to further our own studies by standing on the shoulders of these disappearing giants.

Lamp of Trismegistus is doing its part to help preserve humanity's esoteric history by making some of these classics available to those students who are seeking to unearth the knowledge of these ancient colossi.

So, be sure to check other titles from our *Esoteric Classics* series, as well as our *Occult Fiction, Theosophical Classics, Foundations of Freemasonry Series, Supernatural Fiction, Paranormal Research Series, Studies in Buddhism* and our *Christian Apocrypha Series*. You can also download the audio versions of most of these titles from Amazon, Apple or Audible, for learning on the go.

YOGA

By Annie Besant

Brothers, - In all ages, under every civilization, found within the limits of each religion, there has been an upward yearning of the spirit of man — an attempt to find union with the Divine. It matters not what the special form of religion to which the devotee may belong; it matters not under what particular name he may worship Deity; it matters not, so far as the inner struggle is concerned, in what way he may try to express or to carry out these longings. The significant fact is that the yearning is there, a constant witness to the world of the reality of the spirit, a constant witness of the truth of the spiritual life; the only witness, if you speak with accuracy, of the existence of the Divine, either in the universe or in man. For just as water will find its way through every obstruction, in order to rise to the level of its source, so does the spirit in man strive upwards ever towards the source whence it came. Had it not come from the Divine, it would not seek to rise to the Divine. Were it not that it is the off-spring of Deity, it would not strive to re-unite itself with Deity; and the very fact that the yearning exists, the very fact that efforts, however ignorant, are made to realize it, is the constant and the perpetual witness of the Divine origin of man, is the perpetual proof of that which we were studying yesterday, that the Spark may re-become the Flame; being Flame in its origin, it may expand again into Flame, no matter how cramped it has been within the limits of manifestation.

Now the word *Yoga,* as everyone knows, means "union". It expresses in a single term everything which the Spirit can desire; for in this word "union" is implied everything; as everything comes from the Divine, so union with the Divine means possession of everything — all knowledge, all strength, all purity, all love; and the one word which implies that union marks the highest aspiration which is possible for man. I have said this aspiration is found in every religion. Take one of the most modern of religions, that which is prevalent in the West under the name of Christianity, and you will find there exactly the same attempt towards union that you find carried out so methodically in the most ancient of all religions, the Hindu. The great difference between the two is in the method. You have the aspiration in Christianity; you have not, as a rule, the training; although it is true that within the limits of a single body in the Roman Catholic Church there is some distinct knowledge as to the methods whereby union may be sought. But taking Christianity as a whole, you have aspiration, rather than sustained and deliberate effort. Yet still in reading the lives of the saints, as they are called, you will find from time to time descriptions of a state being reached, which any one amongst you, who has studied the matter, would recognize as identical with the state known to us as that of Samadhi, where consciousness passes upward or rather inward, out of the normal and into the Divine. And although that be obtained as it were by the sheer force of devotion, it is still a testimony that under each religion there is the possibility of union; as indeed we might expect to find, when we remember that all Souls are essentially one, no matter how much they may be divided by differences of birth-place or by differences of religion. And this, it seems to me, is important; important because it testifies continually to the unity that underlies different faiths, and because it tends to break down the wall of separation, which is such a barrier as far as spirituality is concerned, while it is, to some extent, inevitable as long as we remain in the purely intellectual sphere.

But what I should be prepared to maintain, as a matter of argument and of experience, is the enormous advantage of the Hindu religion in that Yoga is there understood in method as well as in object. It is not only that what the Christian calls the "Beatific Vision" is desired, but it is that the method whereby that Vision may be reached is taught, so that the man of the world may, to a great extent, learn the steps which, taken in this life, may in a future incarnation make possible for him an advance in Yoga; while those that are prepared for further advance may, by gaining special instruction, learn step by step that which will take them onwards to the Divine.

Now it is clear that in a lecture like this, which to all intents and purposes is a public lecture — it is clear that the inner side of Yoga must be left practically untouched. Yoga, in the strictest sense of the term, is never taught, save from mind to mind, from Guru to sisya; it is not a matter for the platform, it is not a matter for discussion. Discussion has no place in true Yoga. Discussion belongs to the intellect not to the Spirit; and Yoga is a matter of the Spirit and not of the intellect. So far as the preliminary stages go, we can deal with them from the platform; but the inner heart of Yoga is only for those who, having realized that spiritual truth is attainable, have set their whole heart on the discovery, and who go to seek it, not as controversialists into the intellectual arena, not as disputants who think themselves as good as the one to whom they nominally go as teacher, but who are willing to go to the more highly advanced in spiritual matters to learn in silence and in submission, grateful for every ray of light that comes to them, and who challenge not the light, because the Spirit in them has caught a glimpse of the source whence it comes. What I am going to try to do this morning, is to show you the preliminary stages which will gradually train a man to become capable of seeking instruction in Yoga — to point out to you what you might yourselves find out from your own Sastras as to the published steps — if I may call them so — which lead up to the gate of the Temple; but into the Temple you must go alone to meet there your Teacher; only the pathway which leads to that gate may be shown to you and you may begin to tread it whenever you resolve to do so.

Now in order that you may understand the intellectual side of this process of union, you need to understand your own constitution. That is the first step. It is true that the constitution of man to a very great extent only consists of the instruments whereby he may find himself. Nonetheless must he be able to use these instruments, otherwise the preliminary steps cannot be taken; for, before you can enter on the Path at all, there are certain obstacles that have to be overcome. And those obstacles lie in your own nature; they lie in the constitution of your own being. And these external obstacles must be destroyed before any real progress towards Yoga can be made. An understanding then — which will be intellectual — of your own constitution is the first step you have to take. In studying the constitution of man you need to know it, first from the standpoint of theory and then from that of practice. Because man's constitution may be looked at according as he exists in relation to the different regions of the universe, or according as he can practically divine himself when he desires to investigate these regions. These divisions may be different; but you can learn how they are correlated one to the other.

The divisions are, as I say, first theoretical and then practical. Now the fullest theoretical division is that which you may know as the sevenfold division in man that you may read in any ordinary Theosophical book: you may trace it in your own Sastras, but you will trace it with some difficulty. Because there stress was laid rather on the fivefold division, that being the division of man as he is at present developed, the two higher stages being left out of account, inasmuch as man in his average present condition cannot possibly reach them; and it was thought not desirable at that period to confuse the mind by giving a division which could not be realizable in thought. Hints are however thrown out, so that those who passed beyond the average state of man might be able to seize the knowledge for which they had become ready; and so you will find suggestions, such as that I spoke of yesterday, the "seven-tongued flame". So you will find suggestions of seven vowel sounds; so you will find that Agni is drawn in a chariot with seven horses. So you will find that the great serpent [more often spoken of as five-headed] is occasionally spoken of as seven-headed. In this way you will catch a hint from time to time of something beyond the five — of that fivefold constitution typified by the pentacle, by the letter M, by the Zodiacal sign of

Makara, the crocodile — these will hint to you that while you have these as practical reality ever to learn, there is something beyond if you have the intuition to follow the hints thus thrown out.

Now the sevenfold constitution takes Atman as the Self, which, gradually unfolding, runs outward through the successive envelopes that are only differentiations of the Atman. Thus you get Buddhi, spoken of as the spiritual soul; Manas, spoken of as the rational or human soul; Kama, spoken of as the animal soul, which includes all passions and desires; and Prana, life-principle, circulating through the ethereal body, which is unfortunately called Linga Sarira [Now referred to as Etheric Double or Body] — I say unfortunately, because the same term has a different meaning in the Hindu scriptures. Lastly, the body itself, the Sthula Sarira, the physical and material outside portion of man. That gives you the sevenfold division of man, or the six with Atman as the seventh, Atman being really the whole, but differentiating itself in its manifestation. "It willed, I will multiply".

But come to the division which will be more familiar to many of you, in which man is regarded as Atman, taking on itself five different sheaths — an exceedingly luminous classification, because in each case you have this conception of the sheath that veils the true Self; so that the real process of Yoga will be to get rid of sheath after sheath until the Self stands alone once more as it did at the beginning. According to this, you have for the body the food-sheath, Anna-maya Kosa; you have then, represented in the Theosophical category by the ethereal body and Prana — because the ethereal body is only the vehicle of Prana — you have the Prana-maya Kosa. Then you have the double division which recognizes the duality of Manas, as you will find it taught in Theosophical books, and includes with the lower Manas, Kama, joining together that which after death perishes, and that which passes onward to Deva-loka. So that you have the Mano-maya Kosa, which includes Kamic elements, includes passions and desires, and which takes part in the formation of the body which lasts through the Kama-lokic existence. Next as sheath for the discriminative powers of mind, comes the Vijnana-maya Kosa, thus named from *Jnana,* knowledge, with the prefer *Vi,* implying discrimination and analysis, a process of cutting and breaking up all the separable portions of knowledge, so that it is essentially discriminative knowledge; thus it is occasionally, used to cover over the sixty-four sciences, which are classed together under that name. This Kosa then includes what the Theosophists calls Manas, this discriminative faculty in man, without the argumentative side which belongs to Lower Manas. Then you get the last of the sheaths, the Bliss-sheath — Ananda-maya Kosa — which is Buddhi — for Buddhi is essentially bliss.

Suppose instead of this classification, which deals with man as a sixfold entity, you want to know how man is going to deal with himself when he wants to investigate the different regions of the universe, you find you cannot divine him in this sevenfold or sixfold fashion. The sheaths are not all divisible the one from another. You have to take the division which is only triple. Man can only be divided into three for all practical purposes of Yoga. There are but three Upadhis in which these different principles or sheaths can work; there is the lowest which is spoken of as Stulopadhi; that includes the physical body, but is itself essentially ethereal, because the physical body can be left out of account in this matter; it is has neither part nor lot save that of an obstruction that has to be gotten rid of. The real sense-organs lie in the ethereal body, and the outer casings only appear in the physical body, which to us seems so real. Then you have the Suksmopadhi or the subtle Upadhi that is sometimes described as Linga Sarira, or Linga Deha. It was for this reason that I said it was unfortunate that in the Theosophical nomenclature this name is applied to a lower Upadhi, the astral or ethereal body. This Suksmopadhi is the vehicle for the Kamic and the Manasic principles, and it is in this Upadhi that the consciousness can make itself practically acquainted with the whole of the psychic plane. Then there is the Karanopadhi, which is the sheath really of Atman in Buddhi-manas, and answers to the Ananda - maya - kosa. The permanent body in which what we call the immortal Triad lives throughout the Manvantara. These are the three practical divisions for Yoga, and they are correlated to the three planes of the manifested universe; the Astral plane, of which the physical is only, so to speak, the outer manifestation, so that for practical purposes the physical and astral may be regarded as one. To that the Sthulopadhi belongs. Then there is the psychic plane of the universe; that includes the range of passions and desires and also of intellect. To that Suksmopadhi belongs. Then there is the region above it — the spiritual plane; to that Karanopadhi belongs. So that these three Upadhis are correlated to the three regions of the universe — Astral plus physical — the two as one; Psychic — higher and lower;

Spiritual — the highest. And the practical division is chosen for Yoga, because the consciousness may dwell in anyone of these three planes, and in any one it must have a body, so to speak — a vehicle perhaps is a better word — in which it may dwell. Yoga is not possible save by the existence of these Upadhis in which the consciousness may work in the three great planes of the manifested Kosmos. Yoga brings about the development of these Upadhis and their reduction under the control of the Self, so that it may dwell in one or in the other, may experience the different planes, may unify the whole. For the process of manifestation of the universe is but for the development of this unifying consciousness; the universe exists, it is said in the Scriptures, for the sake of the Soul. All is good Karma that pleases Isvara, all is bad Karma that is displeasing to Him. For Isvara is but the term for the Supreme Spirit, which is one with the Spirit in man. Therefore these Upadhis are developed, in order that in their development perfect union may be secured, and the Spirit may traverse at will every plane of the universe, and have in every plane of consciousness the knowledge which belongs separately to each. That understanding then is necessary for our work.

Now comes the question: how are these planes and these Upadhis correlated with what are called states of consciousness or conditions of Atman? You will find in your Sastras different terms applied according as the subject is taken up from the standpoint of the Atman and the conditions that it assumes, or according as it is studied from without as states of consciousness. Studying states of consciousness you have the three stages, waking, dreaming, deep sleeping; or, to use the technical terms, Jagrat, which is the normal consciousness of normal waking life; Svapna, which is the state of consciousness in what we call dream; and Susupti, the sleep beyond dream — the dreamless sleep we call it. There is indeed a fourth, the Turiya state, but that is not a state of consciousness in manifestation. That is the widening out of the limited consciousness into the all. And therefore it lies beyond this question of vehicles, for in that Atman exists as Atman. It has thrown off every sheath until it has found itself. As long as we are dealing with the Upadhis, with sheaths, we have the three without the Turiya state; no condition remains in the Turiya state. Man may reach it, but he carries thither no vehicle. It is the state of liberation. It is the state which is entered by the Jivan-mukta; but the Jiva either passes finally onwards out of all vehicles, or passing into it as Jiva, pure and simple, returns to the vehicle on leaving it; the vehicle cannot be carried into it; for it is beyond limitation; it is the One and the All. Now turn to the *Mandukyopanisad,* that one which is short, but is so priceless; if you will take it and meditate upon it and find its inner meaning. There you read not of states of consciousness but of conditions of Atman. First comes Vaisva-nara, correlated to the waking state, for in that Atman cognizes the external world. You are told it is in contact with external bodies, that is the nature of this condition. It is then of course in the Sthulopadhi, the lowest of the three vehicles. It passes out of that into the state of splendor, that is the Taijasa condition. In that it studies the internal objects, you are told. The Upadhi for this is the Suksmopadhi; it dwells in the inner world. It passes once more out of that into the state of knowledge, Prajna; then it is said knowledge is uniform; then it is said that its nature is

Bliss, its mouth is Knowledge.

A most significant and luminous statement, worthy of your careful consideration. Its nature Bliss; that implies the presence of the Ananda-maya Kosa. Its mouth Knowledge; that implies, if you will think of it, the suggestion of the presence of that which may become, but is not, the spoken word; the potentiality of the speech belongs to the lower plane. Its mouth is knowledge; the mouth is there, but the nature is bliss; when the Atman comes outwards from that state, then it passes downward into. The realm of speech, and the mouth may utter the spoken word, but there is no word on that plane. There is the potentiality of sound, but not the sound itself. And then there is the fourth. Of that fourth there is nothing said save negatives, for it is indescribable. It is Atman in itself, Brahman in itself. It is the sacred Word as one; no longer as the separated letters. You are given the three letters, A, U, M; each of these being correlated to a condition of the Atman; finally the one — sounded word is spoken; because the Atman has re-become the one and no separation of letters can then exist. So, see even by that outward explanation how much there is of teaching in the printed book. And that is only the outer explanation. You have to find out for yourselves what underlies suggestion after suggestion; but taking it in that form it puts you on the way towards Yoga, for it gives you the three stages, the three steps, the three conditions of the Atman.

And the practical way of realizing those? Of that also we may learn something; although not much when we are dealing with it in a fashion so imperfect as the present. Now let us seek the preparatory stages to make all this theoretical knowledge practical to some extent: at least so far as to make it possible, as I said in the beginning, for the man living in the world with household duties, social duties, and national duties, to prepare himself for the real life. This at least we may take into consideration, with a few hints of what lies beyond. Clearly it will be impossible for a man to spring from the average life of men into the practice of real Yoga. To do that would only mean inevitable failure; for although intense desire might carry a man into the beginning of it, there would never be the tenacity which would hold through the shocks which follow the first enthusiastic springing forward into the inner life. You cannot make a sudden step without an equally sudden reaction. You cannot spring high without the shock of re-descending to the earth. Therefore the wisdom of the ancient sages did not permit a man to enter straightway into the ascetic life. It was forbidden save in the exceptional case where an advanced Soul came into reincarnation, and from birth or earliest childhood special capacities were seen. The ordinary life was a carefully graduated life, in which a man might take up just as much of religion as he felt the inner impulse to take up. The life was a religious life, and religious ceremonies accompanied it throughout, but a man might throw as much spiritual energy as he chose into the ceremonies. He might repeat them as a matter of form, and even then they would remind him of the life beyond the physical; or he might throw into them a little devotion, and then they would lead him a step further; or he might throw his whole heart into them, and they would be a real preparation for the later life. If that were done, if the life of the Gṛhastha — the house-holder — were over, and every duty had been accomplished, then he might pass onwards, if he would, into the life of hermit, to the life of the ascetic; because by these graduated practices he had prepared himself for the finding of the Guru and for the leading of a truly spiritual life.

The first step that is always laid down as a preparation for Yoga is the ceasing from wicked ways. A very commonplace step; a mere truism in every religion; but the fact that it is a truism does not make it less true. And since no Yoga is possible without it, save the Yoga that leads to destruction, the first step is purification of the life and the ceasing from wicked ways. Whosoever has not ceased from wicked ways, thus beginning the Yoga which goes on to the subduing of the senses and of the mind, whosoever has not ceased from wicked ways cannot find Atman. That, then, is the first and most commonplace step, and everyone — if you tell them it is a necessary preliminary — almost every one shrugs his shoulders and says "of course"; but he does not practice it. Until he does, no practice in Yoga is possible. Nothing but talk is possible until a man has begun to purify his life; until he is truthful in thought as well as in speech; until he cannot be persuaded to swerve from the path of rectitude by any outside temptations; until the whole of his thought and desire at least is towards the right, until, however often he falls he recognizes a fall as a fall, and tries to rise again; until he has made at least the attempt to form a righteous ideal and to carry out that ideal practically in life. I say this is the most commonplace of all religious teachings, and the one which is the hardest at first to carry into practice. Now for the enormous majority of men who do not take up this as a rule of life, for the enormous majority Yoga is and can be nothing more than a word; any attempt to practice it is like an attempt to run before learning to walk; and the only possible result is the result which the child has when it is in too much hurry to walk — it falls down and falls down until it learns caution an gains equilibrium.

I say this because there are very many practices which may be learned without purity of life, but these will lead to mischief and not to good. It is far easier to take up a book on Yoga and put into practice for a few minutes, or for an hour or two, or for a day, some particular thing that you may read there, than it is to keep a constant watch over the daily life and purify it at every moment of the day. Far easier, but also far less useful; and the discipline of the body and the mind is the first stage in practical Yoga. In daily life all sorts of methods of discipline may be found, and when a man has really determined to discipline mind and body, he will, through his daily life, as opportunities occur, make for himself some definite rules — it does not matter what the rules are, provided they are harmless — and he will rigidly keep these rules after he has made them. That is to say, he will systematize his life; he will determine certain points of time, and at those points he will force himself to do the things that he has previously decided shall be the occupation of that particular moment or hour. Let me take a very common illustration. He fixes an hour for rising, but when the hour comes somehow he fails to rise. He is lazy, or sleepy, or what not. Now it does not matter in itself whether he rises a quarter of an hour earlier or later than the hour fixed, but it does matter that he shall do what he has determined to do. For the carrying out of a resolution in the face of disinclination strengthens the will — and no progress in Yoga is possible unless the will is strong and the body and mind obedient; this power may be best accumulated in the practice of daily life. And when the mind and body are controlled, brought to obedience, no matter what may be the temptations of sloth or anything else, he has taken the first step on this path of Yoga; for they have been made obedient to something that is higher than themselves. By strengthening the will, the man is making one of the instruments that he is going to use in his further progress. Then take the question of food, not a vital question, but one of considerable importance; you will find certain kinds of food forbidden to those who lead a spiritual life. Food should be correlated to the purpose for which you are living. There is no one rule for everyone which you can lay down for all. There are rules which are different according to the purposes that you are using your life to accomplish. According to that which it is the desire of your life to accomplish, so should be the food that you take to nourish, to keep, the life of the body. Therefore it was that when to be a Brahmana meant to be a man who had made progress in the spiritual life, and who desired to advance rapidly and further along the road, the rules as to what he might and might not do were exceedingly stringent; and then it was that he was told to eat those things that have the Sattvic quality, because he did not want to bring into the body which he was endeavoring to purify any foods having the Rajasic or the Tamasic qualities, which would draw him downward instead of lifting him upwards. It is true that the body is the lowest part of us, but it is not for that fact to be neglected. It is important to lighten your weight if you have climb. Though the weight does not help you upwards, the lessening of the weight will make the upward climbing less difficult than otherwise it would be. And that is all that you have to do in dealing with the body. It does not help you to spiritual life; but it holds you back. And you want to lesson the hold of the body as much as possible. That is really the use of an external observance. If there is nothing but the external, if there is no upward rising, it is almost a matter of indifference whether the weight is heavy or light, for it is always going to remain on the ground, and it is the ground that bears it, and it does not hold anything down. Tie a rock to a post. It does not matter whether the rock be heavy or light, for the post has nothing in it that will rise. But a rock to a balloon which is striving to rise upwards, and as you lessen the weight of the rock, the possibility of rising will come to the balloon, until ultimately the power that draws it upward is greater than the dead weight of the rock that holds it down, and it will go upwards carrying the rock with it, because it has overcome its resistance. That is the way in which the body and all outward observances should be regarded. That is why when the Spirit is free all outward forms become matters of indifferences. The very rites and ceremonies of religion that are binding on the Soul that is still unliberated, become useless when the Soul has gained liberation, for then the Soul no longer can be held by anything. And as the rites of religion are meant to be the wings which will lift the Soul upwards against weight, when the weight has vanished and the Soul is free, it no longer needs these wings. It is in its own atmosphere, where equilibrium has been gained, and neither upward nor downward has any meaning for it; for it is at the center which is the All.

I say this because it a thing that ought to guide your

judgment, if you *will* judge your neighbors. It would be far better if you never judged them at all. What right of judgment has anyone of you as concerns one of your brothers? What know you of his past? What know you of his Karma? What know you of the conditions that surround his life? What know you of his inner struggles, his aspirations and his faults? What right have you to judge him? Judge yourself, but do not judge another; for when you condemn any, judging him only from without and by one or another external observance that he may or may not use, you injure yourselves far more than you injure him; you are judging in the lowest sphere, and you are injuring all your own inner sphere, and clouting it over by the tendency of unkindness and of lack of compassion.

Now it is in connection with this dealing with the body that large number of external observances had been advocated and practiced, — many of them exceedingly useful and some of them exceedingly dangerous. Take a practice which is a very useful one, and which is not dangerous but helpful when practiced in moderation in a country like this, with a very long physical heredity behind it and the practice of thousands of generations; that which is known as Pranayama — the checking of the breath — a practice know to almost every Brahmana at least. This is done with a very definite purpose, with the object of shutting out all external objects and withdrawing the soul from the senses to the mind — the first stage in practical Yoga. The shutting of the various senses physically, these are really lightening, so to speak, of the weight, and making it easier for the mind to retire from the external world. But where these directions, which have been published to some extent, are suddenly taken up by people not fitted to practice them by physical heredity, and when they are carried out with much persistence and with Western energy, without someone, who knows how to guide the student, the practice may become exceedingly dangerous. If it is carried beyond a certain point it may seriously affect the organs of the body and cause disease and death. Therefore, even for you who are Asiatics it is never wise to pursue this practice very far unless you are under the training of someone who understands it thoroughly, and who is able to check you the moment you touch danger. Whereas for the European it is unwise to practice it at all, because he has not any suitable physical heredity, nor are the physical and psychical surroundings amongst which he lives fitted for a practice which may be said to work on the physico-psychical life; thus the practice may be exceedingly dangerous, and for a European who is going to begin, the physical training will begin in a different fashion. There again is a point where judgment would be exceedingly unjust; because unless you take these circumstances into consideration, you may be blaming the man for what? Because he does not do a thing which in him would produce dangerous bleeding of the lungs; and so would entirely take away from him the physical garment in which, if more carefully trained, possibly progress might be obtained.

Of course this may be carried very much further in what is called Hatha Yoga. You may see it carried to the furthest extreme in those cases of the ascetics where some particular practice is adopted — whether that of raising the arm and holding it up till it withers; or clenching the hand till the nails grow into the flesh; or gazing at the sun; or doubling the body, and so on — an enormous number of different practices that some of you must have yourselves seen from time to time. Is there or is there not any value in these practices? How is it that we see them adopted? What is their object and what their real worth? Now it would not be true to say that they are without value. First of all they have this value, that in an age like our own they are constant and standing witnesses to the strength of the inner aspiration which overcomes all bodily passion and all physical temptation in order to seek after something which is recognized as greater than the physical life. It is not fair to omit from sight in judging these cases that service which they do to humanity. For in the world, where almost everyone is seeking after things of the world, where ambition is for money, for place, for power, for fame, for the praise of men, it is not without value that a few should even act in this fashion, and throwing everything that men love aside, proclaim by the very fact of their tortured existence the reality of the Soul in man, and the worth of something which is above the anguish of the body. So that I do not think that anyone should speak lightly of the folly of these men, even though he disagree with them, even though he disapprove of them, even if he say that their method is not right. In any case you should recognize the strength of the devotion which can trample on the body in seeking after the Soul. Even if the method be mistaken, as I myself believe it to be mistaken, still it is a nobler life even in its blunders than the commonplace seeking after transient objects; for it is nobler to seek the higher and climb after it and fall, than it is to seek things only of the earth, to waste everything in gaining those transient objects.

And there is the side, another side, which will bring to them their reward in a future incarnation. It is true they will by these methods never reach the spiritual plane. It is true that by these methods they will never reach the higher spheres of existence. Yet it is also true that they are by these methods developing the strength of will that in their next birth may carry them far along the road. Has it ever struck you what their strength of will must be; not in the stages when the posture has become automatic, but in the early stages, when every moment is a moment of torture? That is the time when the Soul is developed, and when if you pay the price of pain you may purchase that which you pay for. They pay it for strength of will, and that strength of will must come back to them in their future life. And it may be that the strength of will shall then be enlightened by the devotion which made them follow such a life, and that the two together may open up the path towards real knowledge. Although for this incarnation they may fail in reaching the spirit, yet in another devotion and the will combined may carry them far, far beyond those who think themselves wiser, because they are not fanatical, — as I frankly think these men are. You may say to me "Are we to follow the practice?" No; for I have already said I regard it as a mistake. I only mentioned this view because I hear so much of idle scoff, so much of idle jeer, from men who are not to come within a mile of those who have at least recognized and tried to follow the possibility of spiritual life.

And then there is one word to be said of another life, a life which is not of absolute self-torture, but which is that of complete withdrawal from the world to the forest. That has been said to be a selfish life: in very many cases it is connected with selfishness, but not always. Those lives that are spiritual keep up the spiritual atmosphere which prevents the country as a whole from failing as low as it otherwise would. They keep up the recognition of the reality of a spiritual life which may be stimulated into activity, and the fact that India has a possibility of revival in herself is largely due to those recluses of the forests and of the jungles, who have kept possible a spiritual atmosphere into which vibrations may be thrown which then may strike on the outer lives of men.

For what is the underlying truth of Hatha Yoga? It is this; that when growth is complete, body will be the obedient servant of the Spirit, and will be developed along the particular lines which will give to Spirit the organs in the body whereby it may work on the outside universe of Matter. That is the real truth of all Hatha Yoga practices. They train the body. They throw into activity certain centers — certain chakras as they are called — they throw them into activity, and these centers are to act as the organs for the interior life. They are the organs whereby the inner life may work on the material universe, and whereby what are called phenomena may be brought about. Phenomena cannot be brought about by the Spirit at its highest working directly on what we call Matter at its lowest, that is by Atman working directly on the material universe; the gulf is too great, it has to be spanned. And if you are to control the physical universe and physical laws, it is necessary to develop certain material organs and astral organs in connection with the body which, brought into immediate contact below with the physical universe, and in contract above with the mind and

Spirit, will enable the Spirit working downward, so to say, to bring about the physical results that it desires. Now Hatha Yoga is the recognition of this truth and the bringing it into practice on the lower plane. It works first on the body and develops a great many of those organs into control over these inner forces. It makes the body easy to be thrown into a condition which does respond to subtler vibrations, and it subjugates the body.

So one who practices Hatha Yoga can, with comparative ease, obtain control over certain forces of the material universe. It wakes up the astral body, it throws the astral centers into vibration; so that there again, powers are gained of a most extraordinary character, so far as the outer world is concerned. But the powers are bad in the sense — that by beginning from below and stimulating these organs, the physical and astral bodies, without the corresponding action in the mind and the Spirit, the limit of action is soon reached. It is artificial stimulation instead of a natural and evolutionary one. Those organs should be stimulated from above and not from below, if they are to persist life after life; and by the Hatha Yoga practices they are stimulated into action from below, just as in hypnotism you begin by paralyzing the outer senses; thus you gradually lead to atrophy and to permanent paralysis. Hatha Yoga practices, long continued, make Raja Yoga impossible for that incarnation. That is why objection is raised to them in many of wisest of our books. That is why it is said that Raja Yoga is the thing to be sought after and why Hatha Yoga is discountenanced. It is not that no physical practices are ever needed. It is not these psychic powers are not ultimately to be evolved; but it is that they are to be evolved as the natural result of the developing Spirit, and not as the artificially stimulated results of the body first and then of the astral form. To begin at that end means limitation to the psychic plane. To begin on the spiritual means the unifying of all planes into one. That is the essential difference between the two forms of Yoga. Raja Yoga is more difficult and it is the slower, but it is certain. Its powers are carried over from birth to birth, whereas beyond the psychic plane it is not possible to progress by using the purely Hatha Yoga methods.

And now I want to put to you one or two general statements as regards these practices, as I will now call them, that may wisely be used in daily life. You may remember in the *Aitareyopanisad* that after man is formed he is *vitalized* — if I may use a somewhat commonplace expression — by the Devas, and that there the Supreme Soul asks the question: "How shall I enter in?" and he enters in at the place where the hairs of the head divide, that is, the Brahma-randra, the center of the skull. He takes up three places; in the right eye, in the "inner organ", and in heart: three places in which he abides. These places are significant. The right eye stands for the senses; the inner organ for the brain and its mind; the heart for the inner self. And he enters into these one by one, first into the eye, that is, to the senses; then into the inner organ, that is, to the mind; then into the heart, that is, to the final dwelling place in which he resides. That is the keynote to all these triple divisions that I gave you at the beginning. Each of these belongs to one or other of these stages and conditions of which I spoke; and when we begin to practice, it is these that we take up as the stages that may be practiced in the world before the Guru is found; which any one of you may begin to practice, and so make possible for yourselves the later stages when you have succeeded in mastering these. First then in seeking the Soul you will deal with the senses. You may choose some image in the mind, and concentration upon that, until no stimulus can reach you from without. This is the concentration of the mind within itself and withdrawal from the senses. Why should not a man practice this daily? Why should he not get into the habit of being able to withdraw the mind from working in the senses; so that it may be thrown back into itself and work only within the limits of the mind? All great men of thought do it as a matter of natural instinct. All great thinkers do it. Take the thinkers who have given to the world great literary works and read their lives, and you will find that it was a constant fact that when they were occupied with great mental problems they become oblivious of the body; that they would sit thinking, missing their meals, sitting through the whole day, sometimes the whole of the night, oblivious of every want of the body, even the want of sleep, because they had withdraw the mind from the senses and had concentrated it within itself.

This is the condition of all fruitful thought, it is the condition of all fruitful meditation. Meditation is more than this indeed. But this is its first beginning, for you want to draw the Soul away from the senses; otherwise it keeps going outward and you want it to come inwards towards its own seat. Therefore stop the senses. Without that no further progress is possible. And then from the worldly standpoint it will be useful even; for this concentration of mind that you find advocated in old books as a preliminary stage of Yoga, is a condition of the most effective mental work. The man who can concentrate is the man who can conquer the intellectual world; he who can bring all his faculties to a single point becomes one-pointed, as Patanjali has it. That is the one who is really capable of making progress intellectually. You cannot push a wide object through obstacles; you must bring it to a point and it will easily pierce through all. So it is with the mind. If the mind is scattered through the senses it is diffused. There is no propelling force that can send it through obstacles. Bring it to a point, and then the force behind it will push it through. Thus even in common intellectual matters concentration is the condition of success. But this carried out thoroughly brings you to the second stage, the Svapna stage; then the condition is that of the mind being fixed on the internal objects; that is, you will fix the attention on concepts and ideas and not on the objects which gave rise to them. No longer on the outer body but on that which you have drawn from it into the mind; and you study the internal objects, which are the concepts, the ideas, the deductions and abstract thoughts which from the outer world you have collected. The more perfectly you can do it, the nearer you are coming to the completed Svapna stage, and when you can do it well you have really made one stage onward in the Yogic method, for you have gained the power of bringing the soul into the internal organ, and once there further progress may be gained. The next stage, still within the limit of Svapna, is not only to withdraw the mind into itself, but to hold it there against the intrusion of thoughts which you do not desire. Suppose you have already secured it against the intrusion of outside stimuli, and the senses can no longer bring you out of this state of concentration; but perhaps thought can do it. The mind itself may not be thoroughly guarded against such intrusion. It is withdrawn from all possibility of stimulation from without. It may be so strong that a man coming up and touching you would not bring you out of the state of perfect abstraction; but still within itself it may not be equally steady, and an idea may reach it while a sensation cannot. On its own plane a thought may intrude. That is the next stage of concentration. You must be able to kill thoughts. The moment a thought comes, if it is not wanted it must fall away. First you kill it by deliberate action; that is, you reject it when it comes. But the realizing of its presence is lack of concentration. The very fact that you see there shows that it is able to make an impression upon you. Therefore you must deliberately kill it. Therefore when the thought comes to you must throw it back. This will be a long process; but if you keep doing it month after month, nay, year after year, at last it will become automatic, and you will have in the mind such a repellent power that you may set that power going by drawing yourself into the center, and the thought coming from outside and striking against it will get self-thrown back. It is like a wheel revolving very rapidly. If it is slowly moving, any moving body that may come against it may check its revolution. If it is moving very rapidly, any moving body that comes against it will get itself flung off. And in proportion to the rapidity of the revolution will be the force of repulsion with which that body is thrown back. That becomes automatic, and just as you get beyond the stimulus of the senses, you get beyond the reach of the mind: that is, the mind becomes self-centered and the circumference throws off automatically everything which desires to enter. That is the position which you have now secured. There again there is the worldly advantage, for the highly concentrated mind does not wear itself out; it does not allow to enter all the thoughts which it does not require. It does not consider them. It does not allow energy to be wasted on them, and so fritter away its powers. It is kept empty as to thought when work is not required, instead of being a sort of ever busy machine, always going, and so wearing itself out. Instead of this, it is a machine under absolute control, which works or does not work exactly as the Self desires that it shall or shall not.

Beyond this stage no conscious progress is possible without the help of a Teacher. Conscious progress, I say, but unconscious there may be, for the Teacher may be there though you know him not. But there is one way still in which progress may be made, although unrealized in a sense, without your knowing that anyone is helping you, but that is not by knowledge. If you still desire to tread the path of knowledge you must find your Teacher. But there is something in the world which is stronger than knowledge, and that is devotion. For that is the Spirit itself; and while I have been dealing with all that which consciously you can do, there is one other thing that you can also do which will help you. And that is to open wide all the gates of the Soul, so that you no longer shut out the sun, so that the sun of Spirit may stream in and purify and enlighten, without any action of your lower self. Now devotion is the opening of the windows of the Soul. It does nothing. It is an attitude. Devotion means that you realize something which is greater than yourselves, something which is higher than yourselves, something which is sublimer than yourselves, towards which your attitude is no longer an attitude of criticism, no longer an attitude of what you call learning, no longer an attitude save that of prostration, throwing yourself down before it in worship, and remaining silent to hear if any word may come. By that, progress is possible into the innermost recesses of the Spirit, for devotion opens the way for the light to come in; the light is always there, we do not make it. These processes that I have been speaking about are the tearing off of sheath after sheath, so that we may consciously recognize the light. It may seem to get brighter as sheath after sheath is torn off. It does not really get brighter; it is there; but *we* fail in the outer recognition of the light within. Devotion breaks through all sheaths from within; and then the light streams forth; and it has nothing to do but shine. It is the quality of light to shine. It is we who obstruct it, and make its shining out impossible. And therefore it is that in the ignorant man you will sometimes find a spiritual knowledge that transcends the intellectual knowledge that some great genius may have obtained. He sees the heart of things. Why? Because the inner light is streaming forward and the devotion has opened the eye into which light comes, and it sees along the beam right unto the recesses of the sanctuary. Not by knowledge only may be opened sheath after sheath; love too is needed, that the man may find himself, and breaking through them all, one by one, may at last open out the way to the Feet of the God. And that is possible everywhere, not only in forest and jungle, if man can separate himself from the things of earth. For this no outer renunciation is necessary; it is the deeper renunciation by the Soul of all the objects of sense and of the world. It is that which Sri Krsna means when he speaks of devotion. Meditation means this opening out of the soul to the Divine and letting the

Divine shine in without obstruction from the personal self. Therefore it means renunciation. It means throwing away everything that one has, and waiting empty for the light to come in. It means non-attachment to the fruit of action. Everything you do, you do because you are in the world, and your duty is to perform actions. Sri Krsna said, "I am ever acting!". Why? Because if He did not the revolving wheel would stop. So with the devotee; he should do his outer actions, because they are examples to other men; because his Karma has placed him in the world where these duties claim discharge. But it is not *he* who does them. Once devotion is attained, the senses move towards their appropriate objects; mind also moves towards its appropriate objects; but the devotee — he is neither the senses nor the mind. He is the self that is recognized as Lord. And so he is always worshipping, while the senses and the mind are busy with the external and the internal objects. That is the meaning of non-attachment. He is not attached to any of the works which his senses bring about; let them go and to their work, and do it with the utmost perfection. Let his mind also go into the outer world and do its share in the worlds work. It is not himself; he is ever worshipping at the Feet of his Lord. While he is there, external things may do their work; what power of attachment have they to bind him to any of their actions? But to reach that state non-attachment must be deliberately practiced; you must learn to be indifferent to results, provided you do your duty, leaving the outcome in the hands of the mighty forces that work in the universe, and they only ask of you to give them the outer material in which they may clothe themselves while you remain one with them. To do this you must be pure; to do this you must always have the heart fixed on the one reality. The devotee is ever within, in the heart. He is always within the shrine, and the mind and body are busy in the outer world. That is true Yoga; that is the real secret of Yoga.

For all that it is perfectly true that there is a stage in which knowledge once more comes in, and the devotee may learn from his Guru how to become a conscious co-worker with the spiritual forces. He may be a worker before he is conscious of it, only by means of devotion. Conscious co-working implies knowledge. It means that the Guru takes the sisya in hand and teaches him how he may more perfectly purify himself and remain utterly unsoiled by the touch of actions in which he works. While conscious co-working is joy unutterable, co-working at all makes life worth living.

I should not deem it worth while to keep you this morning studying a subject such as this, were it not that it seems to me that one of you here or there may possibly catch some thought of devotion which shall make the way into the inner sanctuary easier and clearer for you than it was before. I have been dealing intellectually with these sheaths of the Soul, intellectually with these regions of the universe, intellectually with these states of consciousness, intellectually with the methods by which progress may be made. I should do less than my duty here to you if I left you on the intellectual plane. Therefore I venture these words as to the essence of Yoga, no matter what the outer form may be; I venture to say to you — to some of you it will seem folly and fanaticism, but what matters that to me? — I venture to say to you that devotion is the one thing that gives security; devotion is the one thing that gives strength; devotion is the one way that opens up the road to the innermost where the Divine is manifest. Better worship ignorantly in devotion than refuse to worship at all. Better bring a flower or leaf to some village God as the poorest of those that come ignorantly and desire to give out of their poverty, than be some great intellectual genius that the world honors, too proud to bow before that which is higher than itself, too intellectually strong to bend its knee before the spiritual life; for Spirit is higher than intellect as intellect is higher than the senses. Spiritual life is the highest life, and it is open to everyone, for the Spirit is the innermost core in each, and none may deny its presence in any man. Cultivate then reverence, reverence for everything which is noble; cultivate worship, worship of that which is divine; and then when the body and the senses fail you, then when the mind breaks down and has nothing more to give you, then that eternal Spirit, which is the life of your life, the Soul of your Soul, That shall rise stronger, because the body and the mind have perished, and going upward it shall find itself — nay, it need not go; it is there already, always — it shall find itself lying at the Lotus Feet of its God: there where there is no illusion, no separateness, no pain: there where all is bliss. For the very essence of the Divine is love and is joy, and that is the heritage of the Spirit, greater than anything that the passing world may give.

THE HATHA-YOGA AND RAJA-YOGA OF INDIA

By Annie Besant

In the first place, allow me to explain why I have chosen this subject for discussion: I have lived in India for 12 years; I have made a fairly thorough study of Indian psychology. I thought it might be useful to speak about these matters of which I have made some knowledge, and which are but little studied by the Western world.

There exists in India a psychological science, the origin of which dates back thousands of years.

It is known that India possesses a very ancient literature. Now, everywhere in that literature we find traces of psychology, and also the exposition of an ancient psychology, in its practical, and not merely in its theoretical aspect.

Since this science has been put into practice for so long a period, is it not reasonable to conclude that there may be in these ideas, these theories, based on repeated experiments, something which may prove useful to modern psychology?

This psychological science of the East is called Yoga, a word signifying to bind, to unite. When we speak of Yoga, we express the idea of forming a union, of binding. Of binding what? Consciousness itself, by realizing the union of the separate consciousnesses of men with the universal consciousness. Yoga includes all the practical methods by which this union may be attained.

Yoga is thus a science which may be both studied and practiced; it is practiced in order to obtain a complete union between the ordinary individual consciousness of man and the super consciousness, by rising from plane to plane, until at last this union is completely attained: then one is said to be free.

In order to understand this science, and also the experiments which I wish to explain, allow me to give a short account of the fundamental ideas on which these experiments are based. It is probable that you will not accept these ideas; but you may, nevertheless, understand them as theories: theory concerning man and, more particularly, theory concerning the consciousness of man. The theory, then, must be understood first of all, in order to be able to explain the aim: otherwise the experiments of the East will always remain unintelligible to the western minds. If you will accept these theories, for the moment, you will understand the *ensemble* of these experiments, and you may perhaps deduce for yourselves conclusions from them which will afford clues with regard to other experiments. Herein lies the value, for western minds — so it seems to me — of a knowledge of this science of the East.

The first proposition is, that consciousness is one and universal. Everywhere, beneath appearances, behind phenomena, a consciousness is revealed; under the diversity of forms persists the unity of consciousness; a unique energy, a unique force, is everywhere in the universe.

This theory may be regarded as closely related to the western conception of one single energy of which all the forces are but the manifestations, the example. But, in India, this energy is always regarded as conscious, that is to say, no division is made between consciousness, life and energy; these are but three words denoting the same essence, but which establish also a distinction between the manifestations of this essence, a distinction which it is useful to remember when experiments are being made. But it must be recognized that this energy is one, and is conscious; is, in fact, consciousness itself.

The second proposition is that this energy, this consciousness — I prefer the word consciousness — manifests itself in the universe through the different forms of matter. The manifestations of consciousness depend on those forms by which it is conditioned. The differences which are perceived are simply differences of form and not differences of consciousness. Consciousness is always present, but it cannot express itself in a complete manner in a restricted form. The evolution of forms depends on this manifestation of consciousness; and when we place side by side consciousness and form, energy and matter, it is consciousness which directs, which is sovereign, which disposes of matter, and each functioning of consciousness creates a form for its revelation. When I use the word "creates", I do not mean creation out of nothing; I mean that consciousness disposes of matter so as to express itself, that all the powers reside in consciousness, but that in order to reveal, to manifest its powers, it is absolutely necessary to find the vehicle of consciousness, that is to say, to organize the material by which it can express itself.

I may on this point quote a very ancient line of a Upanishad, the Chandogya; "The Self, that is to say consciousness, desires to see: the eye appeared; it desired to hear: the ear made its appearance; it desired to think: intelligence was there"; that is to say the efforts of consciousness are shown in obedient matter, directed by that energy which incarnates itself in forms.

You will find the same idea in the physical universe, in the transformations of electricity. You may make different instruments to enable the energy called electricity to manifest, the energy is ever the same, it is only the manifestation that varies. According to the instrument you provide, you can obtain light, sound, heat, chemical dissociations, all these being merely manifestations of electricity, manifestations which are possible because you have provided instruments which afford suitable conditions for each kind of manifestation. But the instrument remains inert without electricity; it conditions the form, it does not produce the energy.

It is the same with consciousness and forms; according to India ideas, if you can fabricate the instrument necessary for the manifestation of an energy, that energy can show itself, and what is called consciousness in men in only a part of the universal consciousness which is found everywhere in the universe, and which is translated into human forms.

But they go further: this consciousness is divided into millions of separate parts called *Jivas* (souls). I do not much care for this word souls — it is quite a theological expression; they are fragments of life, germs, grains of life, sown in matter. The most suitable form of matter is the first veil of the *Jiva,* an intelligent, conscious being; this intelligent, conscious being clothes itself with forms of matter of different degrees of subtlety; these are terms Kosas, a word signifying sheath (the scabbard of a sword, for example), a covering.

There are six of these veils, of these vehicles of consciousness, each coarser than the last. Hence when consciousness thus veils itself and enters into these vehicles which it has to govern, organize and render fit for its functioning, each vehicle of coarser matter detracts from some of its power. In the first and most subtle matter, it can operate freely; in the coarser matter some of its powers are lost. Thus consciousness, enveloped in these veils of matter — which are not yet vehicles for consciousness because they cannot act, which are not yet organized — loses much of its liberty, of its powers, with each additional veil with which it surrounds itself.

I may be asked, why does consciousness clothe itself with these veils? It is because on the highest plane consciousness is vague; it cannot very clearly discern things; it is in the physical body, the vehicle of the coarsest matter, that consciousness can first fabricate the vehicle, of a kind almost perfect, for its manifestation on this plane. Evolution proceeds. Consciousness strives unceasingly to manifest its powers; the *Jiva* works upon the matter, and the vehicles become better and better adapted to its desires.

The man who wishes to evolve more rapidly than by natural processes, adopts methods which have been used for thousands of years, and by which he tries gradually to withdraw consciousness from the coarser material in order that it may function freely in a vehicle of finer material; he endeavors to connect vehicle with vehicle, until he reaches a yet finer vehicle without ever losing consciousness. In this way it becomes possible to perceive worlds composed of subtler matter, and to observe them, as we observe here, scientifically and directly; and afterwards to remember these observations even whilst wearing the coarsest vehicle, that is to say, the physical body. Such are the ideas of the East.

When man is awake his powers are at their lowest; when he withdraws from the physical body in a state of sleep, he begins to act in a world composed of somewhat subtler matter. But when he begins to function there, he is not really conscious of himself; his consciousness is like that of an infant who cannot distinguish between himself and others. But by continuing to function in this way, by repeated experiments, he can attain to self-consciousness on the second plane. If the sleep becomes yet more profound, a yet higher consciousness is revealed, and so on from plane to plane.

Let us note, in passing, that if this theory, proved by many experiments, is true, you have a very lucid interpretation of many of the phenomena of hypnotism and of trance. If it is true that consciousness withdraws from the physical body and functions in a more refined vehicle with enlarged powers, many of these phenomena become intelligible. If, then, you would provisionally accept this theory, it would be possible for you to make some very definite experiments, in order to test the truth of this theory.

I come to another point, and here I am much afraid of clashing with some scientific opinions. It is believed, by those who hold the Indian theory, that man is not the only conscious being in the universe; they believe that there are many other beings besides man who are intelligent, and who are manifestations of the universal consciousness, and that these beings exist in all the worlds; sometimes they resemble man, at other times they do not resemble him. All around us, in space, that is to say in the other worlds which are in relation with the physical world, are multitudes of intelligent consciousness beings, who pursue their lives as we pursue ours; the life is independent, the world is independent, but relations may be established between these worlds.

You doubtless think that you are being transported to the Middle Ages, but these are the India ideas of today.

It is possible for man when his consciousness beings to function in a supra-conscious plane, to get into relation with these beings and even sometimes to make them obedient to his will, because many of these things (beings?) are inferior to man.

I have thought it necessary to tell you this because I wish to relate to you two or three experiences which, to me, are unintelligible without this explanation. If you think that this explanation is not valid, find another; for my part I am incapable of doing so.

There are in India two great systems of Yoga: the Hatha-Yoga, that is to say, union by effort; which begins on the physical plane, and does not lead to great heights; and the Raja-

Yoga, that is to say, the royal union, an entirely mental system, which does no begin with physical practices, but with mental practices. These then are the two great systems; the Hatha-Yoga for the body, the Raja-Yoga for the mind, the intelligence.

Those who follow Yoga are called Yogins. The Hatha-Yogins have two aims; one is to secure perfect bodily health and a long extension of life on the earth; the other is to subjugate, for their own advantage, the entities of the other plane, who are not of a very advanced order. It is usually the Hatha— Yogins who display phenomena. There is much prejudice in India against other races; they mistrust Westerns and are often reluctant to show them phenomena. I have been able to see a great deal because I have lived among Indians, as an Indian. Indians are very proud; they cannot bear that their ideas, their religion, or their theories, should be laughed at.

The Hatha-Yogin forces himself to subjugate completely his body and all the functions of his life. Life is called "Prana", a word usually translated as breath, but it signifies rather, the aggregation of all the powers of life which are found everywhere. The Hatha-Yogin strives to bring under the control of the human will all the vital functions and to render them absolutely subservient to the will. This is done in two ways; the regulation of the respiration, called "Pranayama", a word which means much more than control of the breath, and which signifies control of all powers of life in the body and even outside the body. The second is "Dharana", the perfect concentration of attention and of will on a portion of the body. The results obtained by these methods are wonderful. The so-called involuntary muscles can be controlled. You may convince yourself by a small experiment on yourself that this is possible. You can easily learn how to move your ear by exercising those muscles which are rudimentary in man. The same can be done with all the muscles of the body. It is possible to entirely stop the heart from beating. The movement first becomes slower; then the heart ceases to beat and life is as if suspended; the man becomes unconscious on this plane; then little by little, movement is restored until the heart beats regularly. In the same way, the lungs are controlled, always by keeping the attention absolutely fixed on the part that is to be subjugated to the will. One part of the body after another is thus dealt with. These practices last for years.

The Yogin wishes to obtain perfect health; he desires that all the interior of the body should be absolutely clean. The Yogins make a habit of bathing the interior of their bodies as they do the exterior. They do it sometimes by swallowing quantities of water; but they frequently do it also by reversing the peristaltic action of the intestines; they take in water by the lower orifice and eject it by the mouth. I have seen a man who could that for two or three minutes; he placed himself in water and, after a few moments of these reversed peristaltic movements, he ejected from his mouth what seemed like a fountain of water as long as it was desired that he should do so. This experiment is not beautiful, but is interesting because it shows the power of the human will when directed upon a portion of the body. It is not then surprising that experiments can be carried out with the human body which seem even less credible.

The result of all these practices is a marvelous state of

health, a bodily strength that nothing can break. I have been told — I cannot guarantee this, I am not personally acquainted with an example — that they can sometimes prolong life for a century and a half. Those who have told me this are persons in whom I have the greatest confidence, but, I repeat, I can put forth no proof on this point; what I have observed is the perfect health of these Yogins.

They attain to complete suppression of the feeling of physical paint. It is thus that a man, whose skin is apparently quite sensitive, can lie in a bed of iron points, and yet appear to feel very comfortable; he feels no pain whatever. Similarly, what would ordinarily be regarded as dreadful suffering is not even felt. A man have an arm atrophied by holding it raised for years. Imagine the firmness of a will that can do such things. You can understand that with such a will a man can do what he likes with his body.

These life forces in the body which are half conscious, or what you call the Unconscious, do not constitute an elevated order of consciousness; but they can respond to a higher consciousness, and, in making this response, permit it to control the whole machinery of the body.

This power over the body of suppressing the sensation of pain is found sometimes among those who have not practiced the Hatha-Yoga. One of my friends, of the warrior class, is very fond of tiger- hunting; he is in the habit of going alone in the forest to hunt for tigers; it is in this way that the warrior class hunt tigers. They do not employ elephants or anything that can protect them in their attack; they on foot and quite alone.

One day, however, my friend went tiger-hunting with some Englishmen, mounted on their elephants, as is their wont. At the moment when the tiger attacked the elephant, one of the huntsmen lost his presence of mind, his gun went off and the ball lodged in the leg of my friend who fell. When the surgeon arrived he insisted in putting him under chloroform to extract the ball. My friend refused and said: "I have never lost consciousness and I do not wish to begin now. Besides I shall not feel any pain, you may use your knife". The surgeon demurred, saying; "But if you were to make an involuntary movement it might be very dangerous". My friend replied; "I will not move; if I make a single movement I authorize you to use chloroform". The operation was performed; my friend was entirely conscious; he did not make a single movement. What to another would have been horrible torture, was nothing to him.

Afterwards I questioned him on the subject; I thought at first that it was pride of caste that had prevented his showing the least sense of pain. He said to me: "I assure you that I did not feel the least pain. I fixed my consciousness in my head; it was not in my leg; I felt nothing". He was not a Yogin; but he had this power of concentrating his mentality, which is sometimes found among educated Indians. A hereditary physique is transmitted from generation to generation among those who practice Yoga.

The other Hatha-Yoga which aims at subjugating the beings of another plane, beings always by painful experiments

— the *tapas* — such as the one I have just mentioned, namely, holding the arm raised until it becomes absolutely atrophied. They say that it is possible to develop the powers of the consciousness of a plane superior to the physical plane by these extreme austerities (and they do it), and that they can use these powers of the consciousness of the astral plane — that is what they call it — to make use of the inferior entities of that plane. They can thus obtain *apports* of objects without contract; they can seek what they will, within limits which I will presently indicate; they can do extraordinary things, which here we should call jugglery, but which are done without apparatus, by will power alone, by the aid, as they say, of these *elementals*. Ten years ago, I saw one of these Yogins who wished to display some of his powers. He was nearly naked, a consideration of importance when it is a question of the *apports* of objects. He had no sleeves in which he could conceal things. He wore only a little piece of cloth round his loins; his legs and the upper part of his body — from his waist upwards — were absolutely naked.

He began by one of those feats that can be done here with apparatus, whereas he had only a small table which we ourselves had supplied and a small box with two drawers in it which he allowed us to examine as long and as much as we wished; he had, in addition, an ordinary bottle containing an absolutely clear liquid, like water, but which seemed to me not to be pure water, at least I think not, although I am not sure. We were all seated quite near him; we could touch the table and assure ourselves that it was not a platform which could conceal trickery.

He first said that he wished to show us some *apports* of objects, and that he had *elementals* under his domination. For a moment, he carefully regarded each of those present. He look at me fixedly and said; "You must not interrupt me, nor offer any opposition during my operation". I promised, I assured him that I would remain quite passive. I must tell you that I practiced Yoga myself before going to India; I think this man was aware of it and clearly perceived that I could oppose his amusements.

He asked three or four of us to entrust him with our watches, and he wrapped them in a handkerchief which we lent him. Then he said to us: "I am going to give this parcel to one of you, that you may take it and throw it into the well". This well was in a little courtyard about 50 yards off. One of our party, a gentleman, took the parcel and went towards the well, when another stopped him, saying: "Perhaps we are victims of some trickery; let me assure myself that the watches are really in the parcel". The man who said this was a European and thought that this was simply a juggler's trick; he supposed the Yogin had kept the watches. I do not know where he could have hidden them since he was naked. The Yogin got very angry and said: "Throw the parcel down on the table then". [This anger shows that these men are by no means saints]. One of us opened the parcel; the watches were there. He wrapped them up again, and said: "Give them to Mrs. Besant, who will herself thrown them into the well". I took the parcel in my hands, and I went and threw it into the well.

The Yogin was standing by the table. He raised his arms in the air, his hands were empty. He pronounced some words:

the watches were in his hands.

Explain that as you like; I confine myself to stating the fact. The man said it was his *elemental* who had fetched the watches out of the well. Perhaps you think these things are quite impossible; they will seem to you incredible if you have not been present at spiritistic *séances* where just the same kind of things are done, where objects brought as *apports* without contact. The handkerchief which was wrapped round the watches was quite wet.

The man next suggested cutting off the head of a bird, assuring us that it would not hurt it. I did not wish to witness such a painful experiment. I only wished to see what could be seen without horror. He assured us that he could perform this experiment; but I think that this must be produced by collective hallucination, whilst I do not think that in the experiment with the watches there was any hallucination. And assuredly, there was no hallucination in the following experiment: —

"Ask me", he said "to bring something to you; my *elemental* will bring it in a box". Someone enquired if he could cause objects to be brought from a distant country. "I can if they are in India", he replied, " but it is not possible if the sea must be crossed". Here, therefore, was a limit to his powers. Someone then said to him: "At a distance from a hundred miles from here there is a town where a kind of sweet is made that is found nowhere else in India. Will you bring us some of these sweets?". The man stood in the midst of our circle in full light, it was morning. He opened the box and began emptying it with both hands; he threw some sweets on the table and soon made a pile of them much higher than the box. He said that it was his *elemental* who had brought them. They were really the sweets asked for; we distributed them among the neighboring children, who ate them with much pleasure.

There are but a few of those experiments which are very difficult for Western minds to comprehend, but very easy for an Indian to explain by his theory of consciousness and of the elemental. You might try to make these experiments; perhaps you may succeed, perhaps you may not succeed.

I have been told of an experiment which I have not seen; it is very well known, it is that of the basket and the little child; perhaps I should say that I have seen it once, but I am convinced that it was jugglery and not the effect of Hatha-Yoga. One of my friends, an officer in the English Army, told me that he had seen this experiment performed in the courtyard of his own house. He stood on one side of the basket and a brother officer stood on the other; they saw the child who was put into the basket; they themselves tied with cords; they did not move away from the basket, and they not lose sight of it for single moment. The man was in front of the basket; he began singing in a low voice a strange refrain, which lasted for 10 minutes. After that he proceeded in the usual way. [That is to say, he pierced the basket repeatedly, in every direction, with a sword.] When that was over, and after a great quantity of blood had been seen issuing from the basket, the child appeared amidst the crowd of onlookers safe and sound.

I can only explain that as a collective hallucination. There are things which can be achieved by those who have a more extended knowledge of nature; but on the physical plane, to stick a sword into the body of a child, to shed its blood abundantly and to cause the child afterwards to reappear is impossible, it is contrary to known physical laws. It was his strange chant that induced the collective hallucination. They have very strange chants which produce marvelous effects on the brain; it is thus that they hypnotize a crowd, which sees only what the hypnotizer wills shall be seen.

This experiment, therefore, is not interesting to me; it is fairly easy; it consists in the knowledge of a succession of sounds that hypnotize. This is the secret which is generally in the possession of some family, and is transmitted from generation to generation. Moreover, each family can perform only one kind of experiment, one sort of hallucination.

These Yogins can put themselves into auto-hypnotic trances with great facility; but these trances, when they come out of them, do not seem to leave them with any fresh knowledge; the trance is therefore absolutely useless. I have seen a Yogin who was always in a state of absolute unconsciousness on the physical plane; his disciples took care of him, and fed him; he was like an idiot and had nothing to teach.

These men have developed the power of hypnotizing themselves; but they have not developed the capacity of possessing consciousness on a superior plane which can be transmitted to the brain.

The Yogins can predict the exact hour of their death,

that is to say they can choose this hour. I know one who said: "I will die today at five o'clock". His disciples were with him, at five o'clock exactly he died. They are able to quit their bodies either in a trance, from which they can return, or in death from which they do not return. They generally die in this way, choosing the exact hour at which they wish to quite their bodies.

The other method, the Raja-Yoga, is quite different. There are in Yoga eight successive degrees: Yama, Niyama, Asana, Pranayama, Pratyahara, Dharana, Dhyana, Samadhi; in Hatha-Yoga one begins with the third degree, that is to say Asana, the posture. The posture in which the body is held is of great important in relation to the vital currents. Some of these postures are very difficult, some are quite easy. The Hatha-Yogin assumes very difficult and painful postures. The Raja-Yogin does not as a rule assume difficult postures for the body, but chooses, rather, the easy ones. Patanjali says: "An easy and pleasure posture".

In the Raja-Yoga on begins by the first two degrees, that is to say, by the moral; purification is needful. This is not necessary for the Hatha-Yoga. The first step, Yama, is a negative purification; that is, complete abstinence from all that is evil; not a single creature must be injured, a man must live in perfect charity towards all. The second step is Niyama, that is, positive purification: the practice of the virtues helpful to humanity. Without this there is no Raja-Yoga; these two rungs of the ladder are absolutely necessary. Then a bodily posture must be chosen [Asana] which can be maintained for a long time without fatigue; it is only necessary to keep the back, the throat and the head in a straight line, that is to say, that the vertebrate column should be quite straight in order that the currents may pass without obstacle. The head must not be turned to the right or to the left; to keep the body quite straight is the only position necessary for the Raja-Yoga.

After this comes Pranayama, that is to say, the control of the powers of life in the body. Then the Pratyahara, in which the mind is not concentrated upon one part of the body; but all the mental faculties are gathered together. They are diverted from external objects in order to observe nothing of the environment in which one is placed. All the avenues of sense are closed. At first they are usually closed in a physical manner; there is a way of placing the fingers so as to close at one and the same time the nostrils, the eyes and the ears. But when concentration has been developed, it is no longer necessary to employ these means; the senses cease to function. This is attained simply by mental effort, a method the very opposite of that employed in hypnotism, where the senses are fortified by turning a mirror, for example. This is called collecting the forces, turning the mentality within; there is then perfect concentration [Dharana], not upon one part of the body, but upon an idea; there is a mental image, an image which one must try to make very clear, very precise.

These are the inferior degrees; their object is to liberate consciousness from the body. When the senses no longer function, when the exterior environment has disappeared, when one has become insensible to external contact, consciousness begins to function in a more subtle vehicle belonging to the Beyond; it truly functions; this is what is called in the West the supra-liminal or supra-consciousness. The superior consciousness must work in the world beyond, and make observations; this is termed Dhyana, meditation.

If a yet higher place is reached, one which is called Samadhi [a supra-consciousness which is conscious of itself] it is possible on returning thence to the body to use the physical brain to remember the observations which have been made on other planes.

Such is the conception of the Raja-Yoga, a development more and more intense of the mental powers, complete insensibility to the senses, but perfect interior consciousness.

In this condition the Yoga can vacate his body consciously without losing consciousness, and having left his body can perceive it distinctly lying there as an exterior object beside him. Then the conscious being, who is thus able to regard his body like a cast-off garment, can rise from one sphere to another, make his observations, fix them on the memory, and impress them on the brain, so that they will persist when he returns to the body.

The proof that the body has been really vacated is that knowledge may thus be acquired which is not possessed on the physical plane; and different persons may compare their experiences. Their observations will not be entirely identical, because the play of personality always enters as a factor into the experience, but it is possible to make observations of so precise a kind, that it may easily be perceived that the slight variations in detail are due to differences in the observers, and not to differences in the objects observed.

If you interrogate a dozen persons who have passed at the same hour down the same street, they will tell you very different things; because as the mentality of each person differs, their observations are different. Nevertheless, by their several accounts, even though different, you will have no difficulty in recognizing the street of which they speak.

Thus many persons have been able to observe the same objects in another world and to register their observations when they have returned to the physical body.

If this is possible, it explains many phenomena noted in psychical research. We can understand why consciousness in a state of trance is something much keener, and has a much more extended knowledge than the waking state. If, however, we can have this personal experience of the supra- consciousness, and return to the physical body, we possess satisfying proof and invincible certitude of the persistence of consciousness apart from the physical body.

May I suggest that modern psychologists should make very careful study of the class of experiences called religious; the religious consciousness of monks and nuns and saints is still consciousness. It may be said that it is a deformed consciousness; but sometimes a deformed consciousness exhibits facts of great value.

In India they tell us that the brain is destroyed if it is not trained a certain way before it is allowed to receive the impressions of the supra-consciousness. The brain, indeed, cannot bear, without risk, these intense, rapid vibrations of the supra-consciousness; and before trying these experiments, it is necessary to exercise the brain by thinking the highest and sublimest thoughts. If by intense emotion a man throws himself into the other world, when he returns to his body, hysteria is sure to follow those vibrations; the brain cannot endure these vibrations without preparation, but they can be endured by means of Yoga practices. It has often been stated that those who have given themselves up to these experiments in monasteries or elsewhere, have suffered from lack of sleep or from nervous troubles suggestive of hysteria. That is quite true and I do not wish to deny it; but I say that this is not inevitable. If we proceed step by step, if a strong will creates a suitable condition of the nervous system, the brain may become keener, and at the same time remain absolutely healthy; then you have the Yogin instead of the hysteric.

In conclusion; I have sketched a theory which you can study; You can make experiments in order to discover whether this theory does, or does not, explain the problems that modern psychology cannot solve. The latter collects numbers of facts, but it cannot always explain them. It appeals to the Unconsciousness: but there is not only one Unconsciousness: there is the unconsciousness which is derived from the past, that is, the sub-consciousness; the Hatha-Yogin makes this, too, to become conscious and governs all the movements of the body. Then there is the supra-consciousness, which is the Consciousness of the future, for which the physical body is not yet sufficiently evolved. Therefore experiments with this supra-consciousness present many dangers. It will however be the normal consciousness of the future. Human evolution is not finished; man is still very imperfect; it is possible to put pressure on the body, to make it work in such a way as to hasten the normal advances of evolution. If this is done with precaution, with knowledge, with the help of those who know the way, it is possible to walk along this path without danger, without injuring the body, without becoming a hysteric, without nervous degeneration, and it is just this idea that I have desired to lay before you in this paper.

www.ingramcontent.com/pod-product-compliance
Lightning Source LLC
LaVergne TN
LVHW041459070426
835507LV00009B/683